Step by Step

The Story of Peanut Butter

It Starts with Peanuts

Robin Nelson

Lerner Publications ◆ Minneapolis

Lerner Publications Company
An imprint of Lerner Publishing Group, Inc.
241 First Avenue North
Minneapolis, MN 55401 USA

For reading levels and more information, look up this title at www.lernerbooks.com.

Image credits: David Sacks/Photodisc/Getty Images, p. 3; Maryviolet/iStock/Getty Images, pp. 5, 23 (farmer); pokku/Shutterstock.com, p. 7; mailsonpignata/Shutterstock.com, p. 9; Georgia Peanut Commission/flickr (CC BY 2.0), pp. 11, 13, 21, 23 (shells) (jars); Mailson Pignata/iStock/Getty Images, pp. 15, 17; Vladimir Mironov/iStock/Getty Images, pp. 19, 23 (mix); Jeff Greenough/Getty Images, p. 22. Cover: Roberto Machado Noa/LightRocket/Getty Images (peanut butter); Morrison1977/iStock/Getty Images (peanuts).

Main body text set in Mikado a Medium.
Typeface provided by HVD Fonts.

Editor: Andrea Nelson **Designer:** Lauren Cooper
Lerner Team: Sue Marquis

Library of Congress Cataloging-in-Publication Data

Names: Nelson, Robin, 1971- author.
Title: The story of peanut butter : it starts with peanuts / Robin Nelson.
Description: Minneapolis, MN : Lerner Publications, Inc. 2021. | Series: Step by step | Includes bibliographical references and index. | Audience: Ages 4-8 | Audience: Grades K-1 | Summary: "How does a peanut become creamy peanut butter? Low-level text and fascinating photos help readers learn where peanut butter comes from."— Provided by publisher.
Identifiers: LCCN 2019036557 (print) | LCCN 2019036558 (ebook) | ISBN 9781541597297 (lib. bdg.) | ISBN 9781728401157 (eb pdf)
Subjects: LCSH: Peanut butter—Juvenile literature. | Peanuts—Processing—Juvenile literature.
Classification: LCC TP438.P4 N454 2021 (print) | LCC TP438.P4 (ebook) | DDC 664/.8056596—dc23

LC record available at https://lccn.loc.gov/2019036557
LC ebook record available at https://lccn.loc.gov/2019036558

Manufactured in the United States of America
1-47833-48273-11/21/2019

Peanut butter tastes good!

How is it made?

A farmer grows peanuts.

The sun dries
the peanuts.

The peanuts are picked up.

The peanuts
are sorted.

Machines remove the shells.

C-15

Workers check
the peanuts.

The peanuts
are cooked.

Machines mix the peanut butter.

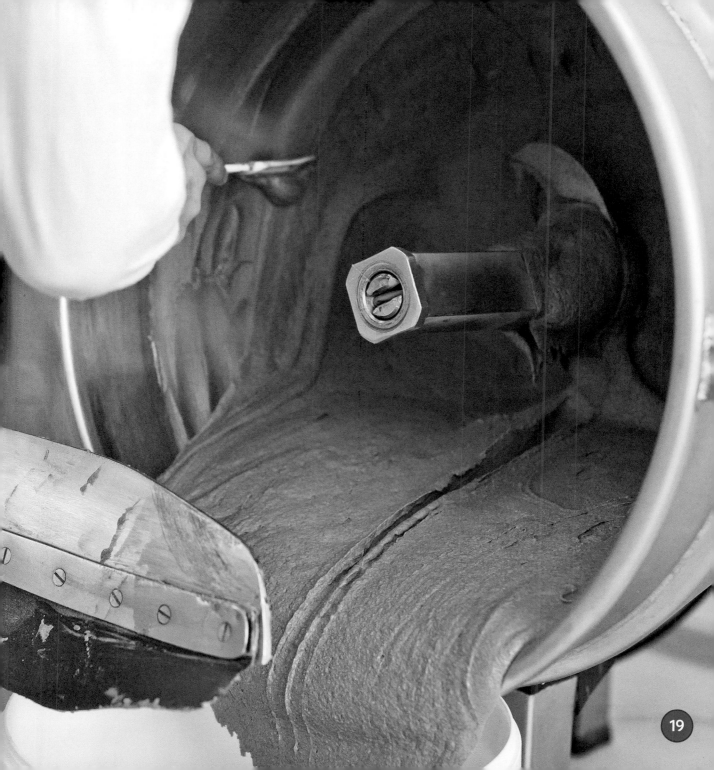

The peanut butter
is put into jars.

Peanut butter makes a great snack.

Picture Glossary

farmer

jars

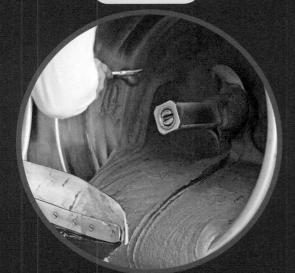

mix

shells

Read More

Bailey, R. J. *Peanut Butter*. Minneapolis: Jump!, 2017.

Heos, Bridget. *From Peanuts to Peanut Butter*. Mankato, MN: Amicus, 2018.

Nelson, Robin. *The Story of Honey: It Starts with a Flower*. Minneapolis: Lerner Publications, 2021.

Index